CPS-Morrill E.S.

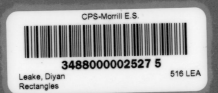

3488000002527 5

Leake, Diyan   516 LEA
Rectangles

W9-ATF-151

DATE DUE

516   BC#34880000025275 $21.36
LEA   Leake, Diyan
         Rectangles

         Morrill E.S.
      Chicago Public Schools
   1431 North Leamington Avenue
        Chicago, IL 60651

Finding Shapes

Rectangles

Diyan Leake

Heinemann Library
Chicago, Illinois

516
LEA
c-1
21.36

© 2006 Heinemann Library
a division of Reed Elsevier, Inc.
Chicago, Illinois

Customer Service 888-454-2279
Visit our website at www.heinemannlibrary.com

All rights reserved. No part of this publication may be reproduced or transmitted in any form or by
any means, electronic or mechanical, including photocopying, recording, taping, or
any information storage and retrieval system, without permission in writing from the publisher:
Heinemann Library, 100 N. LaSalle, Suite 1200, Chicago, IL 60602

Editorial: Diyan Leake
Design: Joanna Hinton-Malivoire
Photo research: Maria Joannou
Production: Chloe Bloom

Library of Congress Cataloging-in-Publication Data

Leake, Diyan.
  Rectangles / Diyan Leake.
      p. cm. -- (Finding shapes)
  Includes bibliographical references and index.
  ISBN 1-4034-7475-3 (library binding-hardcover : alk. paper) -- ISBN 1-4034-7480-X (pbk. : alk. paper)
  1. Rectangles--Juvenile literature. 2. Shapes--Juvenile literature. I.
Title. II. Series.

  QA482.L43 2006
  516'.154--dc22

                              2005013597

Printed and bound in China by South China Printing Co. Ltd

10 09 08 07 06
10 9 8 7 6 5 4 3 2 1

Acknowledgments
The author and publishers are grateful to the following for permission to reproduce
copyright material: Alamy pp. **13** (Rick Yamada-Lapides), **15** (Nic Cleave Photography), **17**
(britishcolumbiaphotos.com); Corbis pp. **12** (McIntyre Photography), **14** (Abbie Enock); Getty Images
pp. **5** (Stone/Erik Von Weber), **16**, **23** (crops, Photodisc; sides, Stone/Erik Von Weber); Harcourt
Education Ltd pp. **6** (Malcolm Harris), **7** (Tudor Photography), **8** (Malcolm Harris), **9** (Malcolm Harris),
10 (Malcolm Harris), **11** (Malcolm Harris), **18** (Malcolm Harris), **19** (Malcolm Harris), **20** (Malcolm
Harris), **21** (Malcolm Harris), **22** (Malcolm Harris), **23** (cuboid, Tudor Photography; hollow, Malcolm
Harris; straight, Malcolm Harris); back cover (card, Tudor Photography; drawer, Malcolm Harris)

Cover photograph reproduced with permission of Alamy

Every effort has been made to contact copyright holders of any material reproduced in this book. Any
omissions will be rectified in subsequent printings if notice is given to the publishers.

The author and publisher would like to thank Patti Barber, specialist in Early Childhood Education,
for her advice and assistance in the preparation of this book.

The paper used to print this book comes from sustainable resources.

Contents

Some words are shown in bold, **like this**. They are explained in the glossary on page 23.

What Is a Rectangle?

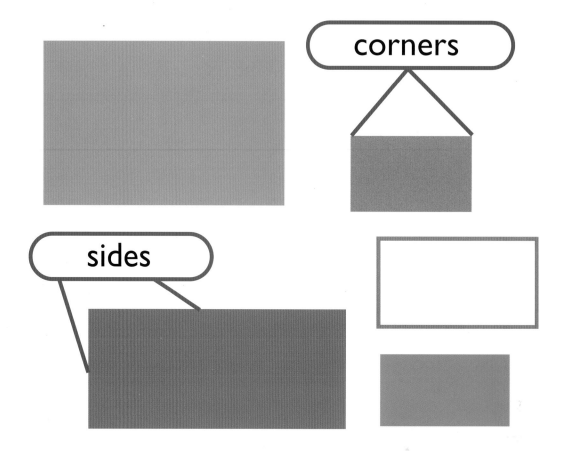

corners

sides

A rectangle is a **flat** shape with four **corners**.

You can see flat shapes but you cannot pick them up.

Rectangles have four **straight sides**.

The opposite sides of a rectangle are always the same length.

Can I See Rectangles at Home?

There are lots of rectangles at home.

Some of them are in the living room.

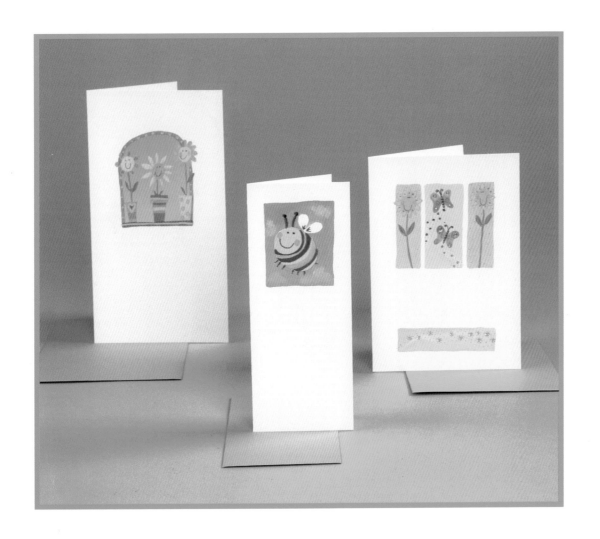

Cards can be rectangles.

What other rectangles are there at home?

There are rectangles in the bedroom.

The front of each drawer is a rectangle.

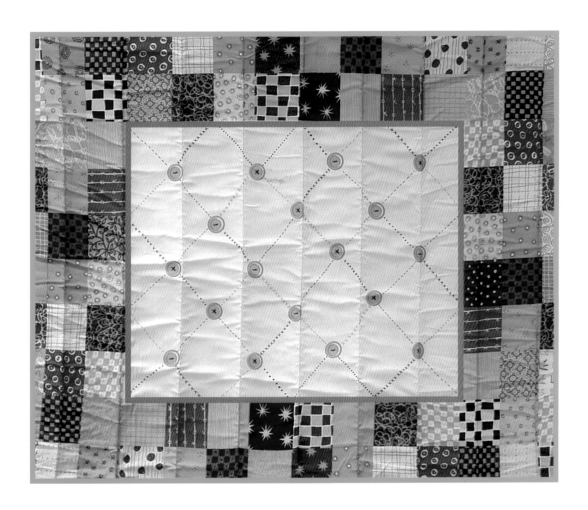

This quilt has a white rectangle
on it.

Can I See Rectangles at School?

There are lots of rectangles at school.

Blackboards and whiteboards are rectangles.

This wall of blocks has rectangles on it.

Some rectangles are long and some are short.

Are There Rectangles Outside?

Some buildings have rectangles on the outside.

This brick school building has lots of rectangles.

You can see rectangles on a climber.

This climber is purple and yellow.

Are There Rectangles in Town?

We can see all sorts of rectangles in town.

The windows on these buildings are rectangles.

There are rectangles in parking lots.

Each rectangle is the space for one car.

Are There Rectangles in the Countryside?

Fields in the countryside can be rectangles.

Farmers grow **crops** in the fields.

These hay bales are in a field.

Each **flat** face of a bale is a rectangle.

Can I See Rectangles on Other Shapes?

faces

Rectangles can be part of a shape called a **cuboid**.

Each face on a cuboid is a rectangle.

You can stack cuboids on top of each other.

Have you ever seen a **hollow** cuboid?

A box is a **hollow cuboid**.

If something is hollow, you can put things in it.

People give presents in boxes.

This teddy bear will be a nice present.

What Can I Make with Rectangles?

Make a pattern with rectangles of different colors!

Picture Glossary

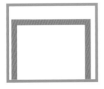
corners
parts of a shape where two sides come together

crops
plants that farmers grow in fields for food

cuboid
shape that is solid (you can pick it up) that has six flat faces

flat
having no thickness

hollow
having space inside

side
outside line of a flat shape

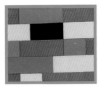
straight
not bent or curved

Index

Note to Parents and Teachers

Reading nonfiction texts for information is an important part of a child's literacy development. Readers can be encouraged to ask simple questions and then use the text to find the answers. Each chapter in this book begins with a question. Read the questions together. Look at the pictures. Talk about what the answer might be. Then read the text to find out if your predictions were correct. To develop readers' inquiry skills, encourage them to think of other questions they might ask about the topic. Discuss where you could find the answers. Assist children in using the contents page, picture glossary, and index to practice research skills and new vocabulary.